Praise the Lord
All the Earth

Patricia A. Purley

Praise the Lord

All the Earth

Copyright © 2022 Patricia A. Purley

All Rights Reserved.

ISBN# 979-8-9870709-0-1

First Edition

All rights reserved. No part of this publication may be reproduced, distributed, or transmitted in any form or by means, including photocopying, recording, or other electronic or mechanical methods without the prior written consent of the publisher.

All Scriptures quotations are taken from The King James Version, New King James Version, New International Version, New Living Translation, and New Revised Standard Version of the Bible.

Evangelist Patricia Purley

36 Four Seasons Shopping Center

Suite 155

Chesterfield, MO 63017

www.blessyourhealth.info

Introduction

I give honor, glory, and praise with Thanksgiving unto God, "The Father for this an even greater opportunity to evangelize, share and spread this Good News Gospel of Christ Jesus. I am honored along with many inspired frontline soldiers, bold and courageous in speaking the Truth of God's Word to see all mankind be set free.

Acknowledgments

I acknowledge and reverence the only true and living God, my Heavenly Father, and my Lord and Savior Jesus Christ, who inspired me to write by the guidance of the Holy Spirit. A Special Thank you to Bishop Patricia T. Whitelock, Minister Nancy Dickson and Evangelist Arquillia Williamson, Editor Dr. Valerie Coates, and my daughter, Trish, for your love, help, support, and dedication to this dream being fulfilled. I am eternally grateful for your efforts. Much love to my sons, Larry, Leon (his wife Sarah), and my precious grandson, Jared, the Body of Christ, family, and friends.

Dedication

I dedicate my life to you, completely, Father God, to fulfill my purpose as a servant of Christ Jesus, being more than a conqueror.

Nay, in all these things we are more than conquerors through him that loved us. For I am persuaded, that neither death, nor life, nor angels, nor principalities, nor powers, nor things present, nor things to come, nor height, nor depth, nor any other creature, shall be able to separate us from the love of God, which is in Christ Jesus our Lord.

Romans 8:37-39 KJV

Make a Joyful Noise unto the Lord all the Earth

The Lord, our Wonderful God, is so good to us, saved and unsaved. God bless us all, which is why everyone everywhere should worship and Praise the Lord with our whole hearts and with gladness. We shall sing our way into His presence with joy.

Father God, help us to know and realize the extraordinary and fantastic privilege and honor you have given us, your people here on the earth. The joy of knowing you, our creator, all belonged to you, and we were created for your pleasure.

The password to enter into your presence is Praise unto our King. Father, you are so good to us. Therefore, we will enter your presence in humility with hearts of thankfulness and offerings of sacrificial worship because we affectionately adore your magnificent and Holy Name.

Oh, Father God, You are so good to us. You're our Provider, Healer, Peace, Hope, Strength, and Way-Maker. You, Father God, are our everything. Your amazing loving-kindness is better than life. What a spectacular, joyful celebration to humbly dwell in your presence every day. Your faithfulness and promises are yes, and Amen to all generations who obey the Word of Truth. Therefore, all the earth should praise the Lord!

Testimony of Psalm 100
Evangelist Patricia. A. Purley

Table of Contents

Chapters

1. Joyously Worshipping Our King
2. I Am Honored to Serve You
3. Singing Praises unto The Most High
4. The Assurance of Who God Is
5. Lord, Mold Me as You Please
6. Our Position of Labor for Harvest
7. Operating in a Spirit of Generosity
8. Bless the Lord in All Things with Gratitude
9. Power of God's Name
10. Celebrating the Lord's Goodness
11. The Need for God's Loving Mercy
12. The Truth that Stands Forever

Chapter 1

Joyously Worshipping Our King

Make a joyful noise unto the Lord all the land.
Psalm 100:1 KJV

The Lord longs to hear from us His creation, His children, in praise and worship. Therefore, as a believer, to make a joyful noise unto the Lord with shouts of joy from the earth consist of praise, worship, singing, and dancing before the Lord playing musical instruments, and many other glorious noises of exhortation.

Shout joyfully to the Lord, all the earth; Break forth in song, rejoice, and sing praises.
Psalm 98:4 KJV

Oh, how I love to shout to the Lord with joy, praise, and worship as I sing songs and hymns throughout the day, no matter where I am or what I am doing. We as believers are always able to joyously express from within the glorious praise and worship with thankful hearts unto our God.

Oh come, let us sing unto the Lord: let us make a joyful noise to the rock of our salvation. Let us come before his presence with thanksgiving and make a joyful noise unto him with psalms.

Psalm 95:1-2 KJV

In the book of Exodus, God blessed Moses, Aaron, and all the Israelites to cross over to dry land while Pharoah and the Egyptians drowned in the Red Sea. When God delivered them out of bondage, Miriam started a celebration unto God.

Miriam the prophetess, the sister of Aaron, took a timbrel in her hand; and all the women went out after her with timbrels and with dances. Miriam answered them, Sing ye to the Lord, for he hath triumphed gloriously; the horse and his rider hath he thrown into the sea.

Exodus 15:20-21 KJV

I recall the powerful praise song of glorious splendor unto our King. Shout to the Lord all the earth let us sing, power and majesty praise to our King, the mountains bow down, and the seas will roar at the sound of your Name.

Stop and reflect on all of God's creation. It is breaking forth into joyous noise of reverence that brings Him glory. Not only His people but the sea roaring, the rivers clapping their hands, and the hills breaking forth in song. Can you imagine the most beautiful picture of all God's creations coming together to worship Him?

It makes you want to shout for joy to the Lord all the earth and burst into jubilant songs with music.
Psalm 98:4 KJV

I always desired to play a musical instrument of glorious worship unto the Lord. So, he anointed my hands to play the tambourine, a joyful noise of worship unto the Lord our King. Worshippers lift their voices as He shines in the light of His Glory, together with the instruments.

Sing aloud unto God our strength: make a joyful noise unto the God of Jacob. Take a psalm, and bring hither the timbrel, the pleasant harp with the psaltery.
Psalm 81:1-2 KJV

We all can relate to the voice of disturbance, distraction, and the common everyday noise of life. However, the message God has given me expresses honor, glory, praise, worship, and reverence. Blessing our wonderful and amazing God creates a joyful noise of declaration of God's glorious name and nature.

The worshipping, singing, clapping, and musical instruments of excellence bring God great glory and honor. All things exist through Christ Jesus, who is worthy. Therefore, I declare a joyful noise unto the Lord as a bold declaration unto his glorious name, arising early, giving Him the first of my day in worship, honoring God, and thanking Him for blessing me to see a new day. I cherish the quiet, intimate times of meditation with my Heavenly Father before I go into prayer. God shall be first in all our priorities; in all, we say and do as His children. We acknowledge worship as a joyful noise or whisper of praise.

Thou art worthy, O Lord, to receive glory and honor and power: for thou hast created all things, and for thy pleasure, they are and were created.
Revelation 4:11 KJV

Believers have the DNA of our Heavenly Father. Therefore, it is the joy of our hearts to bring Jehovah praise. Our Heavenly Father is the Mighty God who rules the sea storms, wild and roaring. With the characteristics to be radical in our praise and worship unto the Lord, His blessed creation, we cannot keep quiet nor keep Him to ourselves.

The floods have lifted up, O LORD, the floods have lifted up their voice; the floods lift up their waves. The LORD on high is mightier than the noise of many waters, yea, than the mighty waves of the sea.
Psalm 93:3-4 KJV

Words of Inspiration:

Shout joyfully to the Lord, all the earth; Break forth in song, rejoice, and sing praises.
Psalm 98:4 KJV

1. We will rejoice in thy salvation, and in the name of our God we will set up our banners: the LORD fulfill all thy petitions.
Psalm 20:5 KJV

2. Speaking to yourselves in psalms and hymns and spiritual songs, singing and making melody in your heart to the Lord.
Ephesians 5:19 KJV

3. Rejoice in the Lord always: and again, I say, Rejoice.
Philippians 4:4 KJV

Reflections:

_____
_____
_____
_____
_____

Chapter 2

I Am Honored to Serve You

Serve the LORD with gladness: come before his presence with singing.
Psalm 100:2 KJV

Father God has created us all for a specific purpose and plan so that our lives bring Him glory. Many things in life cause distractions to turn us from being focused and doing the Father's will. There are many things in life that God has given for us to enjoy. As believers, the greatest priority of our lives is to please God as we live according to His divine assignment. This should be the ultimate priority of our hearts as the Holy Spirit leads us to follow Christ Jesus in obedience.

But seek ye first the kingdom of God, and his righteousness; all these things shall be added unto you.
Matthew 6:33 KJV

In this beautiful, blessed, and bountiful time of miracles in our lives, God is doing remarkable things to bless His people. So many are being saved, delivered from oppression, and the spirit of bondage, healed from sickness and disease, and raised economically as successful business entrepreneurs. God speaks through dreams, visions, and prophetic words. Also, He has equipped us through prayer, fasting, serving, and sharing the Gospel of Christ Jesus in obedience. We must speak the truth of God's words in love to others so that we all may be set free.

In all your ways acknowledge Him, And He shall direct your paths.
Proverbs 3:16 KJV

In the Word of God, Jesus visited His friends: Mary, Martha, and Lazarus, whom He raised from the dead. As Jesus saw this family, the two sisters eagerly prepared for His nourishment and accommodations as they welcomed Jesus into their home. Martha continued to be very busy with preparations and other tasks, concerned that the Lord would be served with the utmost hospitality. While Mary, her sister, sat with Jesus as He shared the Word.

But Martha was distracted with much serving, and she approached Him and said, "Lord, do

You not care that my sister has left me to serve alone? Therefore, tell her to help me.

Luke 10:40 NKJV

Jesus was grateful and appreciative for all that Martha was doing. His visit would consist of an enjoyable meal and fellowship. On the other hand, Mary sat at the Lord's feet, listening to what he taught. Mary enjoyed the servitude of Jesus sharing the Word. She had chosen the best part to sit at Jesus' feet and listen to her master. However, Martha was so occupied with the mundane task of preparing the meal for Jesus. Therefore, Martha remained serving in her natural abilities.

In contrast, Mary chose to be nourished by the spiritual food that Jesus served. For example, Jeremiah stated, "Thy words were found, and I did eat them; and thy word was unto me the joy and rejoicing of mine heart: for I am called by thy name, O Lord God of hosts." Therefore, we must be aware that the presence of the Lord is always around us to hold fast to His truth. We must realize that many things must wait when it comes to receiving God's best plan.

Mary was not going to miss out on the teachings of Christ like Martha.

Although Martha's hospitality was very loving and caring to see that Jesus was served with the best hospitality, our time and relationship with Jesus are the most valuable priority. I learned to put many things aside, meaning we cannot eliminate our responsibilities, tasks, or duties. Instead, we must ask the Holy Spirit to orchestrate our critical, day-by-day responsibilities that need to be done. As believers, there will always be distractions in our life to hinder our time with the Lord. Therefore, all believers must set aside a time of intimacy with God – reading and meditating on His word, fasting, and praying each day. This time with the Lord prepares us for how to serve others.

I thank God that I've learned to discern what is to be taken care of, whether praying, meditating, studying, or reading God's Word. First, as we worship the Lord, we meditate on His love and goodness towards us. Then, as we listen to inspiring testimonials of other believers, we share this Good New Gospel of Christ with others.

Jesus welcomed the love, preparation, and attention to the Word of God given by Mary and

Martha because they served Him with gladness. Yet, the most important thing at that time was quality time spent with the Lord.

But the Lord answered and said to her, Martha, Martha, you are worried and distracted by many things, but only one thing is necessary; for Mary has chosen the good part that shall not be taken away from her.
Luke 10:41- 42 KJV

Jesus positioned himself as a bondservant, an example of a permanent unpaid enslaved person. Becoming a bondservant was the ultimate demonstration of servitude. Nevertheless, precious Jesus, the Son of God, came into the world, willing to obey, giving His life on the cross to die for undeserved sinners.

Who, being in the form of God, thought it not robbery to be equal with God: But made himself of no reputation, and took upon him the form of a servant, and was made in the likeness of men: And being found in fashion as a man, he humbled himself and became obedient unto death, even the death of the cross.
Philippians 2:6-8 KJV

As believers, we, the followers of Christ Jesus, have been called to serve others by the perfect example of our Blessed Savior. He demonstrated His love to many everywhere. He went by pleasing and serving His father through obedience.

As we have therefore opportunity, let us do good unto all men, especially unto them who are of the household of faith.
Galatians 6:10 KJV

As we follow in Christ's footsteps of selfless service unto the Kingdom, this is our calling as we seek to follow His teachings. I humbly accepted Christ as my personal Savior over 35 years ago. As a servant, I have become a front-line soldier to serve and evangelize the Good News Gospel of Jesus. Through prayer, fasting, reading, and studying God's Word, we grow in understanding, wisdom, and knowledge that comes from and through God through His spirit.

Let this mind be in you, which was also in Christ Jesus.
Philippians 2:5 KJV

Serving others without murmuring demonstrates our position in life as faithful servants of God, willing and ready to serve the Lord with gladness. Yet, we may sometimes look at believers as weak and even foolish. Our hurting world needs to know the love of Jesus, who loves us all.

Words of Inspiration:
But God demonstrated his love toward us, in that, while we were yet sinners, Christ died for us.
Romans 5:8 KJV

1. Jesus was always on a mission of obedience to His Father. For Jesus, "Even as the Son of man came not to be ministered unto, but to minister, and to give his life a ransom for many.
Matthew 20:28 KJV

2. If any man serves me, let him follow me; and where I am, there shall also my servant be: if any man serve me, him will my Father honor.
John 12:26 KJV

3. My little children, let us not love in word or in tongue, but indeed and in truth.
I John 3:18 KJV

Reflections:
_____
_____
_____
_____

Chapter 3

Singing Praises unto The Most High God

Come before His presence with singing.
Psalm 100:2 KJV

There is such a significant joy in singing mentioned throughout the Bible. The Old and New Testaments demonstrate the voice of singing throughout humanity. The angels, as well as our Lord, are singing Himself. Although I do not consider myself one who can sing, I will use my voice to sing, worship, and glorify the Lord in song.

Make a joyful noise unto God, all ye lands. Sing forth the honor of his name: make his praise glorious.
Psalm 66:1-2 KJV

Also, singing unto the Lord, a glorious song, took place after the Lord's supper. Jesus and his disciples sang a hymn during the Passover meal. Therefore, we as believers continue to celebrate the Passover meal as a way of remembering the death, burial, and resurrection of our Lord and Savior, Jesus

Christ. So as Christians, we can continue celebrating our Lord's death, burial, and resurrection by regularly taking communion. For whenever we eat this bread and drink this cup, we proclaim the Lord's death till He comes. Therefore, we worship and celebrate as Jesus and his disciples did over 2000 years ago. So, we continue to sing and celebrate.

And when they had sung a hymn, they went out into the Mount of Olives.
Matthew 26:30 KJV

    I can only imagine what Jesus and His disciples sang on such a night of darkness and betrayal. The arrest of Jesus would lead to His trials and crucifixion. I greatly appreciate the celebration as we reverence and reflect on the passion of Jesus and the Glorious Resurrection of our risen Savior.

    O give thanks unto the Lord; for he is good: because his mercy endureth forever. For the Lord loves all His people. Even though the Lord suffered for us, Psalm 118 is a story of God, salvation for all humanity through Christ Jesus, the perfect Passover Lamb. What great love!

The Lord, our God, has a deep and abiding love for us. His people will never know how much God cares and treasures us. He is so concerned about every single thing that concerns us, especially those who have confessed Christ Jesus as Lord and Savior, our Blessed Redeemer who redeemed us from sin. Yes, the Lord celebrates us with shouts of joy. We honor and worship Him as we humbly come before His presence with singing. There are many examples of people singing praises unto the Lord and speaking to one another with psalms, hymns, and spiritual songs.

I embrace the presence of the love of God, worshiping Him in songs as I offer up praise unto Him in the spirit according to the power of His work. I love to sing the scriptures, where God's Word comes alive. It is also one of the most impactful desires of my heart. I am singing God's word back to Him, connecting our hearts to another level of spirituality and intimacy. Singing is significant in the Bible since it has at least 400 references to singing.

David, so skillful in many ways for the glory of God, creates many musical instruments designed for praise. David sang many songs unto the Lord's glory.

The God of my rock; in him will I trust he is my shield, and the horn of my salvation, my high tower, and my refuge, my savior; thou savest me from violence.

2 Samuel 22:3 KJV

The Lord delivered David out of the hands of his enemies as he worshipped the Lord in song. As a child, my ancestors often shared how music and singing were ways to express their feelings, such as joy, inspiration, or hope. So many songs are calming for the soul. Today children of God look for the calming peace only God can give, especially during these challenging times. Despite heartaches and struggles, Christians cannot stop preaching, teaching, and sharing, the hope in Him alone. Our amazing God! Today Old hymns and songs are passed down from generation to generation. During times of slavery, songs were influenced by African Americans, songs of peace, hope, and comfort in Jesus' Name.

Praise ye the LORD. Sing unto the LORD a new song, and his praise in the congregation of saints.

Psalm 149:1 KJV

I end this chapter with the testimony of Mr. Thomas A. Dorsey on how God brought healing and comfort to his heart after the death of his wife and infant son during childbirth. This tragedy caused unbearable grievous pain and grief that only God could heal. Therefore, allow God to heal your heart today, whatever you need. Mr. Dorsey's healing came from the song, Precious Lord Take My Hand, which was the song that God birthed within him.

A Song of ascents:

Precious Lord, take my hand.
Precious Lord, take my hand.
Lead me on, let me stand.
I'm tired. I'm weak. I'm lone.
Through the storm, through the night.
Lead me on to the light.
Take my hand; Precious Lord lead me home.

Lyrics and Music by:
Mr. Thomas A Dorsey

God is concerned about everything that concerns us, His children. Based on research, singing has been shown to bring healing and better health. For example, singing enhances lung function. The controlled nature of breathing in singing increases lung capacity. Also, singing is rehabilitative for people recovering from lung conditions and other known illnesses.

Singing can also help people who are on the road to recovery. Naturally, singing helps build up immune levels and lowers stress hormones. How mindful is the Lord, our God, of how He so graciously created our bodies to worship and sing to His glory? Our bodies are being healed supernaturally by God's miraculous power.

Sing to the LORD, for he has done glorious things; Make known his praise around the world. Let all the people of Jerusalem shout his praise with joy! For great is the Holy One of Israel who lives among you.
Isaiah 12:5-6 NLT

Words of Inspiration:

Sing unto him, sing psalms unto him: talk ye of all his wondrous works.
Psalm 105:2 KJV

1. I will praise thee, O LORD, among the people: and I will sing praises unto thee among the nations.
   Psalm 108:3 KJV

2. Sing unto him a new song; play skillfully with a loud noise.
   Psalm 33:3 KJV

3. Sing unto God, sing praises to his name: extol him that rideth upon the heavens by his name JAH, and rejoice before him.
   Psalm 68:4 KJV

Reflections:
_____
_____
_____
_____
_____

Chapter 4

The Assurance of Who God Is

Know ye that the Lord He is God.
Psalm 100:3 KJV

      God is the Creator and Ruler of the entire universe. He is so great, magnificent, and unique that we cannot fathom how powerful His presence truly is as we love, learn, and know Him and His wondrous works through His word. As I grow in my personal and intimate relationship with Father God, I know that I can trust the promises of God. As His children, when we put our total trust in Him, we can trust Him in all He does, according to His word. He is the Almighty, all-loving, all-powerful, and the Creator of everything. Throughout my life, I've repeatedly experienced the strength God has provided in the lives of the weak- healing the brokenhearted and giving peace to the weary. He has provided for our needs and been our way maker in times of storms. Since He is our everything, we know Him through our relationship to be faithful.

God will do this, for he is faithful to do what he says, and he has invited you into partnership with his Son, Jesus Christ our Lord.
1 Corinthians 1:9 NLT

Despite all the challenges we may experience in life with families, finances, health, and various obstacles, the enemy's attack will try to conform us to the world system if we do not seek God's direction in prayer and fasting. As His children, God even allows storms in our lives. These storms essentially assist us in our divine purpose and rid us of sin in our lives. We can certainly be confident that God is God, by His spoken Word, all He has said and revealed. He is a loving, kind, forgiving Heavenly Father with a purpose for each of our lives.

For I know the plans I have for you says the Lord; They are plans for good and not a disaster, to give you a future and a Hope.
Jeremiah 29:11 NLT

As believers, we recognize and know that "God" is God. We have been drafted into His Royal family. Do you see how much our Heavenly Father loves us? He calls us His children, and that is what we are.

Since we are no longer a part of this earthly world, we must be willing to witness to a world of hurting and dying people. He loves us all so much that He gave His only begotten Son to suffer and die for the sins of the world.

See how very much our Father loves us, for he calls us his children, and that is what we are! But the people who belong to this world don't recognize that we are God's children because they don't know him.
1 John 3:1 NLT

Jesus knew the ways of God. Jesus knew that the Lord God He was God, for He was God and the Son of God.

Jesus answered: "Don't you know me, Philip, even after I have been among you such a long time? Anyone who has seen me has seen the Father. How can you say, 'Show us the Father'? Don't you believe that I am in the Father and that the Father is in me? The words I say to you I do not speak on my own authority. Rather, it is the Father, living in me, who is doing his work. Believe me when I say that I am in the Father and the Father is in me; or at least believe on the

evidence of the works themselves.
John 14:9-11 NIV

We know the Lord. He is God because of His great love for us; He does not need us to be complete, nor does He need us to be whole. He is sovereign; He desires to have a relationship with us and deliver us through His unfailing Love.

I am the Lord your God, which brought you out of the land of Egypt, to be your God: I am the Lord your God.
Numbers 15:41 KJV

As an heir of God, we have not yet received our inheritance, but we are looking forward to and expecting what our Heavenly Father has promised us as His children. As we continue to labor on the earth, we have the power of God's sweet Holy Spirit to operate in his divine authority.

Praise to God, the Father of our Lord Jesus Christ; It is by His great mercy that we have been born again because God has raised Jesus Christ from the dead.
1 Peter 1:3-4 NLT

We know that God is God our Father. As children of God, we can now call him Abba Father, whereby we are not just heirs but joint heirs, meaning that whatever God has given His Son Jesus Christ our Savior, He also gives to us. Because we are children of God, we have many promises from God because of all He endured at Calvary-the pain, suffering, and heartaches.

The Spirit itself beareth witness with our spirit, that we are the children of God: And if children, then heirs; heirs of God, and joint-heirs with Christ; if so be that we suffer with him, that we may be also glorified together.
Romans 8:16-17 KJV

We know the Lord our God through prayer, studying His Word, and a personal relationship. We love and trust God as believers who have confessed Christ Jesus as Lord and Savior so that we all may live a life of purpose through Christ Jesus and the dwelling of His Holy Spirit. His followers demonstrate His Love as we submit unto the Lord with humility. God sent Jesus, our Savior, to redeem us for His purpose.

For God saved us and called us to live a holy life. He did this, not because we deserved it, but because that was his plan from before the beginning of time—to show us his grace through Christ Jesus.

2 Timothy 1:9 KJV

Words of Inspiration:

Behold, what manner of love the Father hath bestowed upon us, that we should be called the sons of God: therefore the world knoweth us not, because it knew him not.
1 John 3:1 KJV

1. In the beginning God created the heavens and the earth.
   Genesis 1:1KJV

2. For God so loved the world that he gave his one and only Son, that whoever believes in him shall not perish but have eternal life.
   John 3:16 KJV

3. Every good and perfect gift is from above, coming down from the Father of the heavenly lights, who does not change like shifting shadows.
   James 1:17 KJV

Reflections :

_____
_____
_____

Chapter 5

Lord, Mold Me As You Please

It is He who made us and not we ourselves.
Psalms 100:3 KJV

    Jesus had a direct focus on the mission Father God gave Him. Even at the age of twelve years old, Jesus was able to identify His purpose by letting His parents, "Joseph and Mary know, that He was in His Father's house, as well as about His Father's business.

And He said to them, "Why did you seek Me? Did you not know that I must be about My Father's business?"
Luke 2:49 NKJV

    God created Jesus, and Jesus came to the earth to save His people from sin with His own life. Because of His death and resurrection, Jesus' great purpose was to restore us.

For this purpose, the Son of God was manifested so that he might destroy the works of the devil.

It is God who has created all humanity with a purpose. We understand the Lord's purpose and how important this is for a fulfilled life in Christ Jesus. As a perfect example, God made us for His pleasure and purpose because we are uniquely created. We are God's handiwork created in Christ Jesus to do good works which God prepared in advance.

For we are his workmanship, created in Christ Jesus unto good works, which God hath before ordained that we should walk in them.
Ephesians 2:10 KJV

God uses us just as He did during the early biblical days. Because His Spirit dwells within us, those who have been adopted into the royal family of God can do extraordinary things.

Read: Acts 9:19-40 KJV

God still uses ordinary Christians today as His humble, faithful, diligent, committed front-line soldiers. People are being saved daily as messengers of the Gospel spread the Word of Truth.

For the Son of man came to seek to save that which was lost.
Luke 19:10 KJV

     Looking at the world's condition today and the purpose God created us. We all know Christ as Lord and Savior, so we may not neglect the opportunities God has provided us as believers to share His Glory and plan of salvation. Regardless of who they are or where they may be, I thank God for the opportunity to witness to the loss in many ways. With the love of Jesus Christ and His Holy Spirit, I correspond, pray, and share literature to reach others in the United States and internationally through my website, post office box, and evangelistic opportunities.

But ye shall receive power, after that the Holy Ghost is come upon you: and ye shall be witnesses unto me both in Jerusalem, and in all Judaea, and in Samaria, and unto the uttermost part of the earth.
Acts 1:8 KJV

     Just as God instructed Jeremiah to go down to the Potter's House to observe how clay pots are made, the Potter takes the clay pots that are messed up and remakes them into better ones. Like clay pots, God is purging us, molding and reshaping us to be more of an example of His perfect Son. As we serve Him here on the earth, we bring Him glory. Just as God told Jeremiah, He is molding Judah and all His people for His purpose and glory.

But now, O Lord, thou are our Father, we are the clay, and Thou our Potter, and we all are the work of your hands.

Isaiah 64:8 KJV

Words of Inspiration:

Before I formed thee in the belly I knew thee; and before thou camest forth out of the womb I sanctified thee . . ."
Jeremiah 1:5a KJV

1. Thy hands have made me and fashioned me: give me understanding, that I may learn thy commandments.
Psalm 119:73KJV

2. Also I heard the voice of the Lord, saying, Whom shall I send, and who will go for us? Then said I, Here am I; send me.
Isaiah 6:8 KJV

3. But we have this treasure in jars of clay to show that this all-surpassing power is from God and not from us.
2 Corinthians 4:7 NIV

Reflections:

_____
_____
_____
_____
_____

Chapter 6

Our Position of Labor for Harvest

We are His people and the sheep of His pasture.
Psalm 100:3 KJV

God instructs us, God's people, who are the sheep of His pasture, to sow and plant spiritual seeds in the life of others so that we will produce good fruits- a field of harvest. We as believers must produce good spiritual fruit- harvesting souls ripe and ready to live for God. We must continue to do Kingdom work through witnessing, serving the less fortunate, and encouraging others in love, joy, peace, long-suffering, gentleness, goodness, faith, meekness, and temperance, demonstrating the fruits of the Spirit. Jesus, "our Lord and Savior, walked and showed these characteristics before us.

As the sheep of His pasture, we walk and live by these examples- not compromising our faith for anyone. But, as believers, we cannot allow ourselves to lose self-control-outburst of anger and other sinful negative qualities that take root in our lives. To win souls for our Lord and

Savior Jesus Christ, our lives before others must exemplify the fruits of the Spirit.

Now the works of the flesh are manifest, which are these; adultery, fornication, uncleanness, lasciviousness, Idolatry, witchcraft, hatred, variance, emulations, wrath, strife, seditions, heresies, envy, murders, drunkenness, revellings, and such like: of the which I tell you before, as I have also told you in time past, that they which do such things shall not inherit the kingdom of God. But the fruit of the Spirit is love, joy, peace, longsuffering, gentleness, goodness, faith, meekness, temperance: against such, there is no law. And they that are Christ's have crucified the flesh with the affections and lusts. If we live in the Spirit, let us also walk in the Spirit. Let us not be desirous of vain glory, provoking one another, envying one another.
Galatians 5:19-26 KJV

We, God's people, who once lived in the bondage of darkness, can rejoice and encourage others to see the light of God. Since Christ saved, healed, and delivered us from the bondage of sin and shame, whereby our lives now represent the character of Christ- others now see and are prayerfully drawn to become followers of Christ. So, we must continue to grow in our faith through the guidance of the Holy Spirit, God's divine helper. Therefore, once lost, we are now sowing seeds of Christlike qualities that lead to eternal life.

That whosoever believeth in him should not perish but have eternal life.
John 3:15 KJV

As a humble, submissive servant of God, I choose to follow and learn the ways of Christ so that I may demonstrate His Love by His Spirit within me. As I trust God, He will continue to cultivate His fruits in each of us. The attitude and actions we live before others during this end-time season will produce seeds- a harvest of souls now and for generations to come.

Let this be written for a future generation that a people yet not created may Praise the Lord.
Psalm 102:18 KJV

There was a story of five wise virgins and five foolish virgins in the Bible. The wise prepared spiritually for the Lord's return but the foolish did not. Some exercised and planted seeds of sinful desires and lifestyles, not preparing for Christ's return. Instead, their roots produced sin that corrupted their character. Still, the wise virgins prepared for Jesus' return by planting good seeds as God's obedient children sowing seeds of preparation for the return of our Lord and Savior, Jesus Christ.

 As I think about my own life as a field of my own planting, what's in my field is determined by the type of seeds I have chosen to sow. I have wasted much of the time in my life that God has graciously given me. I am determined to sow good seeds so that I may reap a harvest of blessings. The greatest blessing is to see souls saved, people healed, delivered, and set free from sickness, tormenting spirits, and serving others. Through prayer, fasting, sharing God's word, and so many other fruits of God's love, we, His people, can demonstrate His righteousness and love and reap the bountiful. Therefore, as believers, we must become a part of a Godly Christian economy stirring up our gifts to be used for the Kingdom of God to help others in these last days.

Be not deceived; God is not mocked: for whatsoever a man soweth, that shall he also reap. For he that soweth to his flesh shall of the flesh reap corruption; but he that soweth to the Spirit shall of the Spirit reap life everlasting. And let us not be weary in well doing: for in due season we shall reap, if we faint not. As we have therefore opportunity, let us do good unto all men, especially unto them who are of the household of faith.

Galatians 6:7-10 KJV

Jesus was always leading by example in obedience to His father. Jesus taught the disciples and others how to love, give, and serve. As a result, no one would be in need as God has called us as believers today to evangelize and stir up the gifts within the community by helping others through the perfect example of Christ Jesus.

They sold their property and possessions and shared the money with those in need. They worshiped together at the Temple each day, met in homes for the Lord's Supper, and shared their meals with great joy and generosity— all the while praising God and enjoying the goodwill of all the people. And each day the Lord added to their fellowship those who were being saved.
Acts 2:45-47 KJV

Read Acts Chapter 2.

Words of Inspiration:

In the same way, let your light shine before others, that they may see your good deeds and glorify your Father in heaven.
       Matthew 5:16 KJV

1. For we are God's handiwork, created in Christ Jesus to do good works, which God prepared in advance for us to do.
   Ephesian 2:10 KJV

2. Being confident of this, that he who began a good work in you will carry it on to completion until the day of Christ Jesus.
   Philippians 4:6 KJV

3. Then saith he unto his disciples, The harvest truly is plenteous, but the labourers are few.
   Matthew 9: 37 KJV

Reflections:

_____
_____
_____

Chapter 7

Operating in a Spirit of Generosity

Enter into his gates with thanksgiving, and into his courts with praise.
Psalm 100:4 KJV

When I think of how blessed I have been and all the people worldwide, the righteous and the unjust will be drawn one day. Although the unbelievers may not yet know Christ Jesus as Lord and Savior, they will be eventually drawn to Jesus by the power of the Holy Spirit, which is being demonstrated from within us, the believers. We once were lost-in sinful darkness but are now found and see that Jesus is the Light of the world. No one comes to the Father except through Christ Jesus, and the Spirit draws them unto salvation. Jesus poured the gift of the Holy Spirit into the lives of every believer. Praise God!

Read John 6

Praise be unto the Most High for such an amazing love for us as sinners. The only way to approach God is through His Son, Christ Jesus, who demonstrated exceptional love through His sacrifice at Calvary. Thank you, Precious Jesus. In all I do, I will always take and spend time with you through prayer, worship, meditation, and serving others. I'm serving Christ through love, praise, worship, thanksgiving, obeying the word, and giving thanks in all things.

Therefore encourage one another and build each other up, just as in fact you are doing.
1 Thessalonians 5:11 KJV

We Praise and revere God for all He has done. Jesus paid the penalty for our sins and clothed us with His righteousness. This sin debt is why we can bring our prayer requests to God in Jesus' Name.

Jesus saith unto him, I am the way, the truth, and the life: no man cometh unto the Father, but by me.
John 14:6 KJV

I give honor, glory, and praise with a thankful heart unto the God our salvation. All creation shall worship Him, for He is the God of our salvation. He is King of King and Lord of Lords whom we must trust and obey as His children. In doing so, we shall live with Him throughout Eternity. Yet, while here on the Earth, we must spread this Good News Gospel among the people so that all will know the Love of Christ Jesus.

O come, let us sing unto the LORD: let us make a joyful noise to the rock of our salvation. Let us come before his presence with thanksgiving, and make a joyful noise unto him with psalms. For the LORD is a great God, and a great King above all gods.
Psalm 95:1-3 KJV

Read Psalm 95

Jesus is our High Priest, Chief Intercessor, Shepard, and Bishop of our very soul, in whom we can confidently draw near to God and bless His name. We can draw near to our Heavenly Father with confidence, knowing that we will receive mercy and find grace in our time of need. We bless the name of the Lord in whose name we pray. As we follow in His footsteps, we ask according to the promises of His spoken Word. and find grace in our time of need. We bless the name of the Lord in whose name we pray. As we follow in His footsteps, we ask according to the promises of His spoken Word.

Within these many years, I have learned that the more I pray, not only as a prayer warrior or intercessor, I experience my prayer life being more effective. As a humble servant, my prayers are answered for His people and my own needs. As I focus on praying and interceding on behalf of others, I thank the Lord that they may know the same love, joy, and mercy God has lavished upon his believers. Now, we as believers are commissioned to show the love of Christ to others-saved and the unsaved, because Jesus paid the sin debt for all humanity.

As a follower of Christ Jesus, I am honored and consider it the most incredible privilege to represent my Blessed Savior in my character, conduct, and conversation while fulfilling His purpose-driven assignment for my life. As believers, God has given us life, time, resources, and much more to live abundantly in Christ. By being reliable and trustworthy to humanity through obedience despite our frailties, faults, shortcomings, and mistakes, we have the gift of the Holy Spirit to teach, lead, and guide us into all Truth.

Howbeit when he, the Spirit of truth, is come, he will guide you into all truth: for he shall not speak of himself; but whatsoever he shall hear, that shall he speak: and he will shew you things to come.

John 16:13 KJV

As I prayed early this morning, I repented for wasted time, resources, and not being sensitive to the Holy Spirit. Our carelessness- past, present, and future, are forgiven when we confess. Therefore, thank God for His loving grace as we pursue our God-given assignment with diligence, integrity, and perseverance, for which we will be held accountable.

Read Matthew 25:14-30 about the talents.

We must always keep the body of Christ lifted in prayer- church leaders, believers, and the unsaved. Therefore, the will of God can be accomplished in each of our lives as we pray for all humanity.

As we have therefore opportunity, let us do good unto all men, especially unto them who are of the household of faith.

Galatians 6:10 KJV

Thank God for the power of prayer and agreement. Our prayer is that the Hope of Heaven remains our focus as believers. We must keep our spiritual antennas up, so we do not get distracted by the enemy's deceptions. Thank God for the keeping power of His sweet Holy Spirit.

Blessed be the God and Father of our Lord Jesus Christ, who hath blessed us with all spiritual blessings in heavenly places in Christ. According as he hath chosen us in him before the foundation of the world, that we should be holy and without blame before him in love.
Ephesians 1:3-4 KJV

Once again, I cannot express my gratitude and heart of thankfulness unto the Lord my God as I praise Him for the Gospel proclaimed as frontline soldiers. God has blessed us as believers to participate in fruitful ministries- spreading the Gospel of Jesus Christ through servanthood.

As we continue to grow in His grace, wisdom, knowledge, and understanding, the Word of Truth will significantly increase as we share with others, no matter who they may be. Therefore, God has equipped us to be a part of a

Christian economy whereby he has planted ministry gifts and talents along with successful business opportunities so that we may be a blessing to the community.

Share your food with the hungry and give shelter to the homeless. Give clothes to those who need them, and do not hide from relatives who need your help.
Isaiah 58:7 NLT

A glorious time of praise, worship, and fellowship is when the saints come together in praise and worship unto the Lord. Many people consider worship service a term often used when people gather to sing and worship the Lord only on Sunday morning. Still, praise is unto the Most High God as believers. Our times of praise and worship shall be much more profound and further than the gathering groups and attendants on Sunday morning. But it should occur anytime and anywhere through an intimate personal relationship with our Heavenly Father- our Lord and Savior Jesus Christ. In our time of intimate fellowship, study, prayer, witnessing, taking communion throughout the week, and sharing the love and goodness of Jesus, "We glorify the Lord in church services, a total spiritual recognition unto God through worship and praise by the power of the Holy Spirit.

God is a Spirit: and they that worship him must worship him in spirit and in truth.
John 4:24 KJV

Ezra and Nehemiah had a great Love for God's people as they attempted to rebuild the temple of the Lord. The Israelites all gave God glory for His love, grace, and mercy towards them. They cried unto the Lord with a great shout of joy and thanksgiving as the rebuilding of the temple's foundation was put in place.

And they sang together by course in praising and giving thanks unto the LORD; because he is good, for his mercy endureth forever toward Israel. And all the people shouted with a great shout, when they praised the LORD, because the foundation of the house of the LORD was laid.
Ezra 3:11 KJV

God alone is worthy of all our praise. We come before God with a thankful heart, acknowledging Him for all he has done and how he has blessed us. We are undeserving of His loving-kindness, sovereign grace, tender mercy, and countless blessings toward us. How can we hold these testimonies of blessings within ourselves? We're to testify to others with joy and adoration unto God as we enter His courts and presence, praising Him with all that is within us. We praise His Holy name.

Now, therefore, our God, we thank thee, and praise thy glorious name.
1 Chronicle 29:14a KJV

The apostle Paul was so grateful unto God for the ministry of preaching, teaching, and sharing the Gospel of Christ as an encourager. He wrote letters to many believers to keep them encouraged. Paul began his letters with thanksgiving as he urged the believers at Galatians, Philippi, Ephesus, the Colossians, and many others. Although Paul started with praise and Thanksgiving unto God and the Lord Jesus Christ in His letters, his letters showed a determination to share the Good News Gospel of God's salvation of Jesus Christ.

Therefore, Paul's life exemplifies how we, as believers, should allow our light to shine. We must continue to spread the Good News Gospel throughout the nations.

Thanks be to God for his indescribable gift!
2 Corinthians 9:15 NIV

Words of Inspiration:

This is the day which the LORD hath made; we will rejoice and be glad in it.
Psalm 118: 24 KJV

1. We give thanks to God and the Father of our Lord Jesus Christ, praying always for you.
Colossian 1:3 KJV

2. Be careful for nothing; but in every thing by prayer and supplication with thanksgiving let your requests be made known unto God.
Philippians 4:6 KJV

3. You will be enriched in every way so that you can be generous on every occasion, and through us, your generosity will result in thanksgiving to God.
2 Corinthians 9:11 KJV

Reflections:
_____
_____
_____

Chapter 8

Bless the Lord in All Things with Gratitude

Be Thankful unto God and Bless His Name.
Psalm 100:4 KJV

I will always bless the Lord, and His praise shall continually be in my mouth. God is the source of all our needs, blessings, and desires. Moreover, God is so gracious and kind that He loves all in whom He has created, whereby His blessings come to all of us even though we are undeserving. For all have sinned and fallen short of his Glory. Therefore, God has commanded us to serve, love, and pray for all humanity, even if they have harmed us or someone else. Consequently, we as believers are to set a Godly example of love before them, giving thanks to God.

But I say to you, love your enemies, bless those who curse you, do good to those who hate you, and pray for those who spitefully use you and persecute you, that you may be sons of your Father in heaven; for He makes His sun rise on

the evil and on the good, and sends rain on the just and on the unjust.
Matthew 5:44-45 KJV

God loves us unconditionally and desires the best for us, His children. Therefore, he is to be highly exalted because of who He is. The King of Kings and He is Lord of lords whom we Thank God for being His, as we magnify His Name forever. Therefore, I will highly praise You, my God, The King, and I will bless your name forever and forever.

I will extol thee, my God, O king; and I will bless thy name forever and ever.
Psalm 145:1 KJV

I consistently seek God's best for my life as I strive to live the life in which He, My Heavenly Father, has created within me despite my frailties and the difficulty of a pure, perfect, and complete holy life. Yet, I desire to inspire, encourage, and serve others. I am thankful to God by His Spirit. He expects an attitude of study, learning, and growth from the Truth of His Word. Blessed be the Name of the Lord from this time forth and forever. The Lord's name is to be praised from the rising of the sun to the going down of the same.

Blessed be the name of the LORD from this time forth and forevermore.
Psalm 113:2 KJV

God blesses us all, believers and unbelievers, because of His unconditional love. We all matter to Him and have much to be thankful for, especially His sovereign grace and mercy.

I testify that no one can do us like Jesus, providing for our life now and forever. God provided a completely pure, once-for-all-sacrifice, eternally freeing all humanity from the guilt of sin. Our sins are taken so seriously by God. Society may take sin lightly, which is why the world is suffering. God has made the way through His Son. All He requires us to do is repent, repent, repent. God provided this permanent sacrifice for all humanity to deal permanently with their sins. We are thankful for Christ going to the Cross and paying our sin debt once and for all. Thank God there will never be a need for another sacrifice for sins. The Blood of Jesus Christ wipes the record clean forever. Hallelujah! Amen!

For God's will was for us to be made holy by the sacrifice of the body of Jesus Christ, once and for all time.
Hebrews 10:10 NLT

Read Hebrews 10:1-18 NLT

     Long ago, when the sacrifice of animals was made in the Old Testament, the Lord graciously allowed the people to offer an animal sacrifice to substitute for humanity. This temporary solution that God allowed had to be repeated and repeated, being the only sin debt payment at that time. But God offered up His precious Son, Christ Jesus. No other animal sacrifices were needed, especially when humanity was the guilty one. Being thankful unto God who provided the perfect and sinless sacrifice of Christ Jesus, who set us free from our sins whereby we have Eternal life in Him, the all-sufficient One.

For the wages of sin is death, but the free gift of God is Eternal Life in Christ Jesus our Lord.
Romans 6:23 KJV

God Bless us so that we may be a blessing to serve, give, and share with others, especially the less fortunate. As God speaks, leads, and guides us through the Holy Spirit, He also instructs us to forgive so that we may strengthen one another.

O bless our God, ye people, and make the voice of his praise to be heard.
Psalm 66:8 KJV

Naturally, anyone saved and unsaved should want to give to the poor, less fortunate, to poverty-stricken areas, for Jesus said they will always be with us. It's just a blessing as God taught us, the believers, through his Son, Jesus, by demonstrating how to give and serve others.

Thanks to the Lord always, for it is He who continues to pour out blessings upon us all. We are so thankful to the Lord, our wonderful God. We cannot help but bless his matchless name.

Bless the LORD, O my soul. O LORD my God, thou art very great; thou art clothed with honour and majesty.
Psalm 104:1 KJV

It is my honor to serve the Lord and do His will as I serve others by evangelizing and sharing the Good News Gospel of Jesus Christ. He blesses us to have all we need to help, serve, encourage, and show compassion and love for others as we glorify the Lord. In doing so, he blesses us both spiritually and naturally.

Bless ye the LORD, all ye his hosts; ye ministers of his, that do his pleasure.
Psalm 103:21 KJV

We are setting our minds on the things above where Christ, our Savior, intercedes on behalf of God. Therefore, our attention, affections, and abilities follow His plan for our lives. For it is God's Kingdom and righteousness that should direct our plans, pursuits, and pleasures. Therefore, God has given me- goals and even Godly dreams for my life to pray, encourage, and speak to others, confirming what God has given us. If we follow the Spirit, it will indeed work for our good.

And we know that all things work together for good to them that love God, to them who are the called according to his purpose.
Romans 8:28 KJV

The Angels of the Lord are mighty in strength. The Angels of the Lord are on assignments from God in our lives. For example, the Angel of the Lord blessed Mary, the mother of Jesus our Savior, with that important message from God that she would conceive the gift of our Savior by the Holy Spirit. I, too have encountered miracles from God through ministering angels: delivering the message of guidance, protection, and instructions. So, God sent a Host of Angels to the lowly shepherd while tending their flocks in the field to go and greet Mary, Joseph, and baby Jesus, our newborn King. God sends angels to us, all of whom we are unaware of their divine presence.

Do not neglect to show hospitality to strangers, for by doing that some have entertained angels without knowing it.

Hebrews 13:2 New Revised Standard Version

As my personal testimony, I worship, praise, thank God, sing to Him, quote scriptures, and pray throughout the day and night. God sees fit to put me back to sleep at His time, giving me visitations of dreams on many occasions. Oh, how I love His Name! I am thankful for how God demonstrated the power of His amazing Love for me with a portion of life, health, strength, and salvation through Christ Jesus. He is our provider: providing peace, protection, and healthy, blessed children and family members. We also possess Godly wisdom, knowledge, and understanding of our Creator God and our Lord and Savior, Christ Jesus, as we continue to learn, study, and meditate on His word. These promises are available to all who would believe and receive. Therefore, we, the believer, should not be anxious about anything. We trust God to completely control our lives as we share this magnificent Good News Gospel with others, praying for others and leaving all our cares in the hands of the Lord. He knows our request, even before bringing our petitions before Him. God desires communication in prayer and intimacy of fellowship before our Heavenly Father. Thank you, Lord.

Blessed be God, which hath not turned away my prayer, nor his mercy from me.
Psalm 66:20 KJV
The Apostle Paul expressed thanksgiving and gratitude for the most significant spiritual

gift any believer could imagine. That is the spirit of Christ in us, the Hope of Glory. We are so grateful that as we make our heavenly deposits toward kingdom work, God's children will not be bankrupt before our Lord. My personal testimony is to continue to move and allow the Holy Spirit to lead as I surrender my will unto the Father through Christ Jesus, which is more important than any world ambition or priority.

Read Colossian 3

Jesus performed many miracles during His time here on the earth. Ten lepers cried out to Jesus to heal them. Only one returned to say thank you. Therefore, we must let Jesus know how grateful we are for all He does and our gratitude toward one another each day. Yes, of course, we know that he is omnipresent, knowing all things simultaneously, but to hear us speak from our mouths and express gratitude from our hearts honors the Lord, our Savior.

After they were healed, the ten lepers were ready to return and resume life as usual, but one came back to express His gratitude and thankfulness unto Jesus for healing him.

And one of them, when he saw that he was healed, turned back, and with a loud voice glorified God.
Luke 17:15 KJV

Read Luke 17:11-19 below.

And it came to pass, as he went to Jerusalem, that he passed through the midst of Samaria and Galilee. And as he entered into a certain village, there met him ten men that were lepers, which stood afar off: And they lifted up their voices, and said, Jesus, Master, have mercy on us. And when he saw them, he said unto them, Go shew yourselves unto the priests. And it came to pass, that, as they went, they were cleansed. And one of them, when he saw that he was healed, turned back, and with a loud voice glorified God, And fell down on his face at his feet, giving him thanks: and he was a Samaritan. And Jesus answering said, Were there not ten cleansed? but where are the nine? There are not found that returned to give glory to God, save this stranger. And he said unto him, Arise, go thy way: thy faith hath made thee whole.

Words of Inspiration:

Saying, Amen: Blessing, and glory, and wisdom, and thanksgiving, and honour, and power, and might, *be* unto our God for ever and ever. Amen.
Revelations 7:12 KJV

1. Lift up your hands to the sanctuary and bless the Lord.
   Psalm 134:2 KJV

2. Giving thanks always for all things unto God and the Father in the name of our Lord Jesus Christ.
   Ephesians 5:20 KJV.

3. Bless the LORD, O my soul, and forget not all his benefits. Who forgives all your iniquities, Who heals all your diseases.
   Psalm 103:2 KJV

Reflections:

_____
_____
_____
_____
_____

Chapter 9

Power of God's Name

And Bless His Name
Psalm 100:4 KJV

There are so ways we, the believers, can bless the Name or even the many Names of God. These names accommodate every need we may have. Every Name of the Lord is mighty. We, the righteous, can run to the Lord. We bless Him because of His Name, Elohim. Therefore, we, his people, are safely shielded and protected as He carries us through times of difficulty. When we hollow His Name, we bless his entire character, representing his love and nature: what an incredible God, creator of all things.

In the beginning, God created the heavens and the earth.
Genesis 1:1 KJV

Abba Father is the most intimate form of God's Names. We bless His Name for being our Father God, our loving Daddy. God cares about all that concerns us. Our Heavenly Father gives His children the strength and covering we need for this life's journey. Therefore, we have the assurance that when His children call, He will answer.

And because ye are sons, God hath sent forth the Spirit of his Son into your hearts, crying, Abba, Father.
Galatians 4:6 KJV

There are so many superior and extraordinary Names by which the Lord our awesome God is known. So, when there are tragedies, chaos, and circumstances beyond measure in the natural, we call on his name. However, in the supernatural, we call on El Shaddai, God Almighty, in whom we find rest.

He that dwelleth in the secret place of the most High shall abide under the shadow of the Almighty.
Psalm 91:1 KJV

As Jesus grew up in wisdom and knowledge, he proceeded to go forth and do the will of the Father. He continued the work that His Father purposed Him to do. As the Son of God, He ministered to all who chose to believe and follow His ministry. In doing so, we will receive eternal life through Jesus Christ. God's precious Son in whom he was well pleased.

For whosoever shall call upon the name of the Lord shall be saved.
Romans 10:13 KJV

Everyone who believes in Christ knows Him as Lord and Savior. His very Name is precious and higher than any other Name. Oh, how my heart rejoices with expectation as I try to reach as many as possible who may not yet know Christ Jesus as Lord and Savior. One day, we will look for those who believe in God to be in heaven, bow before Him, and give an account of the life we have been given here on earth.

For we must all appear before the judgment seat of Christ; that everyone may receive the things *done* in *his* body, according to that he hath done, whether *it be* good or bad.
2 Corinthians 5:10 KJV

For this reason, God sent Jesus to teach the early church about the truth of God's Kingdom, a government in heaven that will bring peace to all the earth. This peace comes from knowing Christ Jesus as Lord, who provides hope for everything in life.

And let the peace that comes from Christ rule in your hearts. For as members of one body, you are called to live in peace. And always be thankful.
Colossians 3:15 NLT

As believers or anyone who desires true happiness and peace, we can indeed find it in Christ Jesus, who is our perfect example. Jesus showed us how to walk in God's will even when it seemed impossible under challenging circumstances. Therefore, Jesus did not retaliate when He was mistreated. He is the Prince of Peace, and His peace dwells within us to walk in peace with all humanity through the power of the Holy Spirit.

Thou wilt keep him in perfect peace, whose mind is stayed on thee: because he trusteth in thee.
Isaiah 26:3KJV

We were called because Christ suffered for us, leaving us an example we should follow in His steps. He did not sin, and no deceit was found in His mouth. When they hurled their insults at Him, He did not retaliate. When He suffered, He made no threats. Instead, when God's children call out the specific name of the Lord in worship and praise, our Jehovah Jireh provides for our every need. Jehovah Nissi fights our battles, and Jehovah Rapha, He is the God that heals us. For God is our everything; he is eternal and unchangeable.

And God said unto Moses, I AM THAT I AM: and he said, Thus shalt thou say unto the children of Israel, I AM hath sent me unto you.
Exodus 3:14 KJV

The name of God is Elohim; Elohim means God. This name of God refers to His incredible power and might.

A few of God's names and titles are below.

Elohim, My Creator
Jehovah- My Lord God
El Shaddai- My Master
Jehovah Jireh- My Provider
Jehovah Rapha- My Healer
Jehovah Nissi- My Banner
Jehovah-Tsidkenu- My righteousness

Jehovah Shalom- My Peace
Jehovah Roi- The Lord is my Shepherd.

Therefore, God is the only true and living God, our Creator, the mighty one of Jacob. God is the Heavenly Father of all believers. God's actual name is Yahweh, the God of the Israelites, the Hebrew Name revealed to Moses.

And Moses said unto God, Behold, when I come unto the children of Israel, and shall say unto them, The God of your fathers hath sent me unto you; and they shall say to me, What is his name? what shall I say unto them? And God said unto Moses, I AM THAT I AM: and he said, Thus shalt thou say unto the children of Israel, I AM hath sent me unto you. And God said moreover unto Moses, Thus shalt thou say unto the children of Israel, the LORD God of your fathers, the God of Abraham, the God of Isaac, and the God of Jacob, hath sent me unto you: this is my name forever, and this is my memorial unto all generations.

Exodus 3:13-15 KJV

God is the highest, which means no idol god or created being may be worshiped or exalted above the Lord because He is superior.

Therefore, the Lord alone is the highest priority of our praise and worship, who rides the cloud as we rejoice in his presence.

Sing unto God, sing praises to his name: extol him that rideth upon the heavens by his name JAH, and rejoice before him.
> **Psalm 68:4 KJV**

Rejoice in His presence.

  I have a special blanket with all the Names of the Lord our God, our precious Lord and Savior Christ Jesus on it. Each Name has a significant powerful meaning representing the nature of God's love. The Names of the Lord are just as important today as in the early Biblical times. His many names are why he deserves the highest praise.

That at the name of Jesus every knee should bow, of things in heaven, and things in earth, and things under the earth; And that every tongue should confess that Jesus Christ is Lord, to the glory of God the Father.
> **Philippians 2:10-11 KJV**

Christ is the Messiah, meaning the most powerful Name of Jesus. Jesus fulfilled all the Old Testament prophecies about the Messiah's first coming. The remaining Messianic prophecies will be fully realized when Christ Jesus returns to reign as King on earth. Therefore, I pray that all will answer the call, determining eternal destiny by choice. Jesus stands ready to receive all who answer the call of our Great and Mighty King.

Forasmuch as there is none like unto thee, O LORD; thou art great, and thy name is great in might.
Jeremiah 10:6 KJV

Words of Inspiration:

For unto us a child is born, unto us a son is given: and the government shall be upon his shoulder: and his name shall be called Wonderful, Counsellor, The mighty God, The everlasting Father, The Prince of Peace.
Isaiah 9:6 KJV

1. The name of the LORD is a strong tower: the righteous runneth into it and is safe. **Proverbs 8:10 KJV**

2. Blessed be the name of the LORD from this time forth and for evermore. **Psalm 113:2 KJV**

3. Let them praise the name of the LORD: for his name alone is excellent; his glory *is* above the earth and heaven." **Psalm 148: 13 KJV**

Reflection:
_____
_____
_____
_____
_____

Chapter 10

Celebrating the Lord's Goodness

For the Lord is good.
Psalm 100:5 KJV

At one time, so long ago, I did not understand nor realize that God had a great purpose for my life when He allowed me to endure trials and hardships. However, my spiritual growth continues to be developed through life challenges when I refuse to fall into despair and discouragement. However, on occasions, even when my faith wavered, His love brought grace and mercy.

For thou, Lord, art good, and ready to forgive; and plenteous in mercy unto all them that call upon thee.
Psalm 86:5 KJV

When I look back on many of the trials I endured in my life, they turned out to become an overwhelming blessing of abundance. I know many saints, including myself and even the Apostle Paul, who pleaded with the Lord to remove the burdens, which is a natural feeling.

However, Father God left the thorn in Paul's flesh, for His grace was sufficient. God is good in any event.

Another reason I wrote you was to see if you would stand the test and be obedient in everything.
2 Corinthians 2:9 NIV

We must not become impatient and feel we can fix things ourselves as Abraham and Sarah did. They never doubted God's goodness. But instead, their faith wavered, and they lost patience.

Scripture Reading: Genesis 15-18.

Through spiritual growth and maturity, I've learned by the Holy Spirit to acknowledge that some trials have overtaken me. These trials established a temporary foundation. But, according to God's good plan and purpose, his marvelous works direct and guide us all.

The LORD is good to all: and his tender mercies are over all his works.
Psalm 145:9 KJV

Though I may not always understand God's plan, one thing is sure. I have learned to go with the spiritual flow through prayer, fasting, waiting, and speaking God's word. Therefore, I have learned to trust the Father and cooperate with God. He knows everything from the beginning to the end. Consequently, He is good, and His plan for our lives is good.

Thou art good, and doest good. Teach me thy statutes.
Psalm 119:68 KJV

When the Israelites were delivered by God out of Egypt and safely crossed the Red Sea, God also miraculously moved the waters in the Jordan river for their safe passage. They overcame obstacles that would hinder their victory toward entering Jericho. The Lord God Almighty was so good to the Israelites, repeatedly demonstrating His love, faithfulness, and compassion.

The LORD is good, a stronghold in the day of trouble; and he knoweth them that trust in him.
Nahum 1:7 KJV

Writing down my dreams, God's miracles, and blessings in my life is a constant reminder of God's goodness. I experience victorious outcomes, and more extraordinary doors of opportunities have brought me significant spiritual growth and Godly wisdom. Therefore, I humbly submit unto God, who has performed His good works through other believers and me.

Being confident of this very thing, that he which hath begun a good work in you will
perform it until the day of Jesus Christ.
Philippians 1:6 KJV

I do not have to see or know God's specific plan for my life or the people I pray for each day. Instead, I have learned that God's goal is to use our hardship for good, and we must remain humble with thanksgiving in our hearts. As time passes, God's people become more mature in the things of God.

And we know that all things work together for good to them that love God, to them who are the called according to his purpose.
Romans 8:28 KJV

Jesus perfectly represented the Good News Gospel when He explained and demonstrated just how good God is. He took all our sins upon Himself and instructed us to follow Him. Jesus brought all humanity great joy through the Good News Gospel. We can read about it, study it, and live what we confess as we share this Good News with everyone so that none will be lost, but all shall be saved.

Neither is there salvation in any other: for there is none other name under heaven given among men, whereby we must be saved.
Acts 4:12 KJV

There are many beautiful testimonies to God be the glory. Even though many experiences have been painful, God causes them to work out for our good without a doubt. If God were not good, no one would have been promised eternal life through the suffering of the cross. God brought great comfort through Christ Jesus as we trust and are moved by his Holy Spirit. As a more significant purpose unfolds before and within us, all who trust God will experience His great plan for each of our lives.

Every good gift and every perfect gift is from above, and cometh down from the Father of lights, with whom is no variableness, neither shadow of turning.
James 1:17 KJV

Words of Inspiration:

I am the good shepherd: the good shepherd giveth his life for the sheep.
              John 10:11 KJV

1. Oh, taste and see how good God is.
   Psalm 34:8 KJV

2. Trust in the Lord, and do good; so shalt thou dwell in the land, and verily thou shalt be fed.
   Psalms 37:3 KJV

3. Surely goodness and mercy shall follow me all the days of my life: and I will dwell in the house of the Lord forever.
   Psalm 23:6 KJV

Reflections:

_____
_____
_____
_____
_____

Chapter 11

The Need of God's Loving Mercy

His mercy is everlasting.
Psalm 100:5 KJV

We stand in awe of our God's grace and mercy so that we may live totally dependent on Him. It is all about God's goodness and His favor on His people. As we labor for the Gospel, we are assured of His loving grace from within us.

But whatever I am now, it is all because God poured out his special favor on me—and not without results. For I have worked harder than any of the other apostles; yet it was not I but God who was working through me by his grace.
1 Corinthians 15:10 NLT

I am personally grateful for God's consistent, loving concern to meet my needs and the needs of His people. It is a natural routine to pray for the just and even the unjust throughout the day. As believers, the Lord our God guides our steps when we obey and continue to listen.

He forgives our sins, comforting and strengthening us in our hardships. Oh, the joy of the Lord lavishes His grace and mercy upon us with divine favor that we certainly do not deserve. As a child of God, we are taken care of by our faithful Heavenly Father while on earth. The eternal ages to come are promised the boundless riches of His loving mercy and grace.

Scripture Reading: Ephesians 2

The Apostle Paul was overwhelmingly grateful for God's everlasting mercy and sovereign grace in His life through His ministry to the early church. As Paul continues to encourage us through the Word of God, we, the believers today, are also recipients of the mercy of God and certainly have his blessings. Paul often started or ended His letters by speaking of God's loving grace. Paul experienced the power of God's divine grace and mercy that transformed his life and enabled his service unto the Lord. Whereby Paul was also able to endure adversities with joy and contentment. Paul knew God's divine grace was sufficient. God strengthened his weaknesses through Christ Jesus. No matter what Paul endured, it would not take his peace nor joy because he was secured by the Love of Christ Jesus resting upon him.

But he said to me, "My grace is sufficient for you, for my power is made perfect in weakness." Therefore, I will boast all the more gladly about my weaknesses, so that Christ's power may rest on me.
2 Corinthians 12:9 NIV

      In our flesh, there dwells nothing good. God's sovereign grace shows love through our weaknesses, frailties, and faults. Because we are saved and born-again believers of Christ Jesus, He actively produces His love through us. Therefore, the fruits of the spirit are the only way righteousness will be seen in our lives. As we abide in Him, we must trust him to purge, mold, and wash us, which is the process known as sanctification. God's grace is working to complete us in Him.

      Remain in me, and I will remain in you. For a branch cannot produce fruit if it is severed from the vine, and you cannot be fruitful unless you remain in me.
John 15:4 NLT

God's mercy and grace are and forever will work in our lives. Just as our salvation never ends, God's promises are sealed unto the day of redemption and will not grieve God's precious Holy Spirit.

The LORD will perfect that which concerneth me: thy mercy, O LORD, endureth forever: forsake not the works of thine own hands.
Psalm 138:8 KJV

I love the story of Bartimaeus. He was the beggar that Jesus healed his eyes of blindness. Along with Bartimaeus over thirty years ago, my eyes were headed towards complete and total blindness. A condition called Retinitis Piagmentosa, which man cannot cure only God. The eyewalls have been damaged to the point where they will cause blindness.

Nevertheless, my eye specialist and other specialist are puzzled and find it hard to understand. Once they dilated my eyes and saw the condition, their diagnosis was blindness. Excuse me while I give Jesus, my Lord and my Savior Jehovah-Rapha, my Healer, some praise! The same mercy the Lord showed toward blind Bartimaeus is God's same mercy toward me.

When He called me out during a revival service in California, he restored my sight from total blindness. What I deal with now is nothing compared to not having any eyesight. The assignment that God had purposed for my life will be accomplished with or without sight. That is why I will never stop thanking the Lord my God and giving Him glory for His mercy in this and many areas of my life, unto His glory. Nothing in my life, just as it was in Bartimaeus or any believer's life, deserves God's mercy. Because of the nature of God, he responds to our every need since we are His beloved children. Just as Christ Jesus poured out his blood over the mercy seat, we all may receive grace and mercy through the sacrifice of our Lord and Savior Jesus Christ.

And when he heard that it was Jesus of Nazareth, he began to cry out, and say, Jesus, thou son of David, have mercy on me.
Mark 10:47 KJV

Thank you Lord for your Grace and Mercy.

Scripture Reading: Mark 10:46-50

God is indeed a God of mercy, while He is also a God of justice. God's wrath is against sin, lust, evil desires, impurity, sexual immorality, and greed. God offers salvation to all, and we will all stand before the judgment seat of Christ to give account for our lives while here on earth.

For we must all appear before the judgment seat of Christ; that everyone may receive the things done in his body, according to that he hath done, whether it be good or bad.
2 Corinthians 5:10 KJV

As believers, we have fallen short of the Glory of God. For His glory is His fullness and goodness; we reverence His presence, meaning there is no possible way for any of us to reach the presence of God or achieve the high standard of His goodness. God's glory is the ultimate desire of us, the believers, for He alone is worthy.

For everyone has sinned; we all fall short of God's glorious standard.
Romans 3:23 KJV

We, as believers, admit our sins before a holy God in humility. Through immediate prayer and repentance, God is a God of justice. He will forgive and cleanse us of all unrighteousness when we accept Christ Jesus as our Lord and Savior by faith. God then responds by His grace and mercy. What a wonderful, loving, and caring God we serve. God's righteousness is provided to sinners as a gift. Because He loved us so much that our sins demanded death, God sent Jesus as our substitute upon the cross. His love and mercy paid our sin debt.

And to wait for his Son from heaven, whom he raised from the dead, even Jesus, which delivered us from the wrath to come.
1 Thessalonians 1:10 KJV

After Jonah finally completed the assignment, God commanded him to go toward Ninevah. Once Jonah delivered the message from God, Jonah described God as being gracious and compassionate. God is slow to anger and abounds in love while holding back disaster from overtaking them.

And he prayed unto the LORD, and said, I pray thee, O LORD, was not this my saying, when I was yet in my country? Therefore I fled before unto Tarshish: for I knew that thou art a gracious

God, and merciful, slow to anger, and of great kindness, and repentest thee of the evil.
Jonah 4:2 KJV

Scripture Reading: Jonah Chapter 4

O give thanks unto the LORD; for he is good: because his mercy endureth forever. Let Israel now say, that his mercy endureth forever. Let the house of Aaron now say, that his mercy endureth forever. Let them now that fear the LORD say, that his mercy endureth forever.
Psalm 118:1-4 KJV

    If you do not know Christ Jesus as Lord and Savior, this invitation is crucial and offered throughout this book. First, we all can come to Christ Jesus for the forgiveness of our sins so that we may be reconciled to the Heavenly Father. Then, as believers, we can continue to feast and partake of spiritual sustenance. He provides as we continue to share this Good News Gospel of Christ Jesus.

Seek ye the LORD while he may be found, call ye upon him while he is near.
Isaiah 55:6 KJV

Scripture Reading: Psalm 1

Words of Inspiration:

Let us therefore come boldly unto the throne of grace, that we may obtain mercy, and find grace to help in time of need.
Hebrews 4:16 KJV

1. But God, who is rich in mercy, for his great love wherewith he loved us.
   Ephesians 2:4 KJV

2. But go and learn what this means: 'I desire mercy, not sacrifice.' For I have not come to call the righteous, but sinners.
   Matthew 9:13 KJV

3. I beseech you therefore, brethren, by the mercies of God, that ye present your bodies a living sacrifice, holy, acceptable unto God, which is your reasonable service.
   Romans 12:1 KJV

Reflection:
_____
_____
_____
_____

Chapter 12

The Truth that Stands Forever

And His Truth endures to all generations.
Psalm 100:5 KJV

As I grew in my faith, I realized this took time, study, and sacrifice. As a result, I now know my Savior better and learn more each day about how to live a life pleasing to God and living the life He has purposed and created.

For I know the plans I have for you," declares the LORD, "plans to prosper you and not to harm you, plans to give you hope and a future.
Jeremiah 29:11 KJV

I am living the best days, the latter days of my life, as I try to live a life to please God, which is rewarding, for a life of purpose is worth it all. A life dedicated to God is only possible by God's Spirit and through the obedience of God's Truth.

O that my ways were directed to keep thy statutes!
Psalm 119:5 KJV

I desire to please and glorify God to overcome sin, worries, and fear. Therefore, I stay before God praying and interceding for all humanity. However, once we become children of God and followers of Christ Jesus, prayer, studying, and meditating on God's word, must be our ultimate and most significant priority. The Word of God instructs us as His children to grow in His word.

Dear children, let us not love with words or speech but with actions and in truth.
1 John 3:18 KJV

I realized the importance of following God's instructions on many occasions and organizing my thoughts. However, once you think you have it together, you find it does not work because our attention sometimes drifts away from God's instruction. We feel we know enough to continue the task by our instruction, which results in a disaster.

I seek you with all my heart; do not let me stray from your commands.
Psalm 119:10 NIV

The Bible

Before leaving the Earth, the believer's instruction is God's instruction to all who are born again. The truth of God's word is not to be ignored, which becomes dangerous. Without God's Word of guidance concerning truth, reading and studying every day brings us to a standstill in our Christian life. We began to drift toward our plan and not the ways of God. As a result, our plans and dreams will eventually lack the spiritual wisdom to grow in our faith. Therefore, blind distractions will cause many to fall and stumble into a ditch of confusion.

Give me understanding, and I shall keep thy law; yea, I shall observe it with my whole heart. Make me to go in the path of thy commandments; for therein do I delight.
Psalm 119:34-35 KJV

As I pray, read, and study the Bible, my love for Jesus grows. He is the center of my life, joy, peace, and every wonderful thing possible, even through the things I have suffered. It is He who made way for me. Therefore, through our Lord and Savior Jesus Christ, I have learned to love, obey, serve, and proclaim His good news no matter who I am around or where I may be. It is all about Jesus and our relationship with Him and the Holy Spirit that works from within us. To God be the Glory!

Jesus saith unto him, I am the way, the truth, and the life: no man cometh unto the Father, but by me.
John 14:6 KJV

I pray that my lifestyle is a godly example before others each day, no matter what anyone says or thinks. My goal is to please God. The Holy Spirit is my teacher, Helper, and Guide, which God has given to all believers throughout each day.

But the Comforter, which is the Holy Ghost, whom the Father will send in my name, he shall teach you all things, and bring all things to your remembrance, whatsoever I have said unto you.
John 14:26 KJV

I thank God for my testimony of how the Holy Spirit helps me remember God's Word. As I think and meditate on what I am reading or have read, I apply it to my life, sharing it with others as I am led. For example, God's Word of

Truth is powerful, which He spoke from the beginning of the early church and even now.

Study to shew thyself approved unto God, a workman that needeth not to be ashamed, rightly dividing the word of truth.
2 Timothy 2:15 KJV

There is a passage of scripture for every occasion of life's situations. God's Word is the sure foundation. I have learned to grow and depend on God. Even when life seems chaotic with so many challenges, we can trust the truth of God's Word that He speaks and promises through men inspired by Him to say what God Himself has told, and His word does not change. We are inspired by the Holy Spirit that equips us to go forth. By applying the Holy Spirit and living a life of obedience to our everyday life, God's plan will be carried out in our lives according to His timing, will, and purpose. As His children are helpless and totally dependent on Him, what He promises is in His Word.

This book of the law shall not depart out of thy mouth; but thou shalt meditate therein day and night, that thou mayest observe to do according to all that is written therein: for then thou shalt

make thy way prosperous, and then thou shalt have good success.
Joshua 1:8 KJV

I am the first to say that there is so much I do not understand about God's Word. Yet God reassured me through my time studying with Him and my willingness to learn. God's word is my life. If He says it, I believe it, and that settles it. Nowhere can I be considered any scholar as the Apostle Paul was. However, the Bible was written for all humanity to follow the instructions and plan of God obediently.

Thy word have I hid in mine heart, that I might not sin against thee. Blessed art thou, O LORD: teach me thy statutes.
Psalm 119:11-12 KJV

We read and listen to God's Word to gain and grow in the wisdom, knowledge, and understanding of the teachings of Christ Jesus. Jesus taught His disciples in parables. Just like today, his followers must apply the Truth to their lives. As God brings us in contact with whom we must share the word of God, I have served in California and Missouri in many ministries- Foster Care, Shriner's Children, Nursing Home, and street ministry, along with my daycare and various children ministries. God has given me to evangelize and share the Good News Gospel of Jesus by serving humanity. Those who will take heed and listen and the generations to come; by faith, we trust and believe God's Word to touch, save, and heal lives.

So then faith comes by hearing, and hearing by the word of God.
Romans 10:17 KJV

I long for my intimate, personal, and quiet time with the Lord, as any believer does, with a desire to grow in respect to our salvation. We long for the indwelling of the gift of God's precious Holy Spirit that teaches, guides us, and brings comfort through the truth of God's Word.

As newborn babes, desire the sincere milk of the word, that ye may grow thereby.
1 Peter 2:2 KJV

I have learned to spend quality time with the Lord and His word to prioritize things to grow in my faith as I share His truth with others. As we speak His truth in love, all humanity willing to listen and obey will be set free.

Therefore, we must keep a stronghold on the promises of God's Word by speaking and sharing God's Truth.

He must have a strong belief in the trustworthy message he was taught; then he will be able to encourage others with wholesome teaching and show those who oppose it where they are wrong.
Titus 1:9 NLT

The Word of God reminds us that His anger is nowhere near the anger of us as humans. God's very nature is love. He is merciful, gracious, and good. His wrath is the just and measured response of His holiness towards evil and sin. God's wrath is provoked.

Remember, and forget not, how thou provoked the Lord thy God to wrath in the wilderness: from the day that thou didst depart out of the land of Egypt until ye came unto this place, ye have been rebellious against the Lord.
Deuteronomy 9:7 KJV

God is slow to become angry at us, His people. This self-control is because of the unconditional love for Israel, showing grace and forgiveness repeatedly over us today through

Jesus Christ. In the world today, where there is so much sin, injustice, cruel acts of evil, ungodliness, and unrighteousness before a Holy God, we as believers are to cry out like never before, trusting the promises of God in His Word.

For the wrath of God is revealed from heaven against all ungodliness and unrighteousness of men, who hold the truth in unrighteousness.
Romans 1:18 KJV

David defeated his enemies by God's power and strength, which God assured David with the wisdom to do because God's hand was upon David. In every battle, struggle, and circumstance, we have the promises of God through His word.

So they came up to Baal – Perazim David said, "God has broken in upon my enemies by my hand like the breaking forth of waters: therefore they called the name of that place Baal-Perazim.
1 Chronicles 14:71 KJV

God has given us power and authority over the wiles of the wicked. Nevertheless, some matters will cause our emotions to become upset without sinning. Righteous indignation was demonstrated by the Righteous Judge our Savior when the people violated the temple of God the Father.

Be ye angry, and sin not: let not the sun go down upon your wrath.
Ephesians 4:26 KJV

And Jesus went into God's temple, cast out all them that sold and bought in the temple, overthrew the tables of the moneychangers, and the seats of them that sold doves, and said unto them, "It is written, My Temple shall be called the house of prayer, but ye have made it a den of thieves!"
Matthew 21:12-13 KJV

When we read, study, meditate, live, share, and believe God's Word of Truth through scriptures, we shall prosper significantly in every area of our lives.

Scripture Reading: Psalm 119:33-40 KJV

I genuinely thank God and meditate on His, of Truth and all believers who will listen to our Heavenly Father's sound doctrine. He will certainly show us the best path to walk through any circumstances. I certainly have many, many testimonies of the promises of God. His answers did not always come instantly or without effort on my part. By continual prayers, I trusted God's Word as I prayed His Word of Truth, meditating and thanking God for past victories. God's faithfulness never failed.

My times are in thy hand: deliver me from the hand of mine enemies, and from them that persecute me.
Psalm 31:15 KJV

     I accepted Jesus into my heart and made Him the Lord of my life thirty-nine years ago. My life has never been the same as I share this Good News Gospel of Jesus with others. I am now a child of God. The angels in heaven rejoice to all who will accept this remarkable gift God has so graciously made available to all who would accept Christ Jesus as their Lord and Savior. Amen!

That if thou shalt confess with thy mouth the Lord Jesus, and shalt believe in thine heart that God hath raised him from the dead, thou shalt be saved. For with the heart, man believeth unto

righteousness; and with the mouth, confession is made unto salvation.
Romans 10:9-10 KJV

If you do not know Christ Jesus as Lord and Savior, pray to receive Him today as your personal Savior. If you do know Christ Jesus as Lord and Savior, care enough to share.

Receive Christ Jesus today by confessing Him as Lord and Savior. Repent, and be baptized every one of you in the Name of Jesus Christ. For the remission of sins, you shall receive the gift of the Holy Ghost. The promise is to you and your children even as many as the Lord our God shall call.

Then Peter said unto them, Repent, and be baptized every one of you in the name of Jesus Christ for the remission of sins, and ye shall receive the gift of the Holy Ghost. For the promise is unto you, and to your children, and to all that are afar off, even as many as
the LORD our God shall call.
Acts 2:38-39 KJV

Pray with a sincere and trusting heart.

Dear God in Heaven,
I come to you in the Name of Jesus to receive Salvation and Eternal life. I believe that He died on the Cross for my sins and that God raised Him from the dead. Therefore, I now confess my sins and accept Christ Jesus as my personal Savior. Amen.

Words of Inspiration:

I have no greater joy than to hear that my children are walking in the truth.
3 John 1:4 KJV

1. He that walketh uprightly, and worketh righteousness, and speaketh the truth in his heart.
   Psalm 15:2 KJV

2. And ye shall know the truth, and the truth shall make you free.
   John 8:32 KJV

3. Guide me in your truth and teach me, for you are God my Savior, and my hope is in you all day long.
   Psalm 25:5 KJV

Reflection:

_____
_____
_____
_____
_____

Inspirational Healing: Evangelist Patricia A. Purley

Beloved

I wish above all things that you prosper and be in health even as your Soul Prosper.

3 John 1:2 KJV

You are welcome to contact Evangelist Patricia Ann Purley for prayer, and spiritual literature.

36 Four Seasons Shopping Center

Suite 155

Chesterfield, MO 63017

Email: jc1177pap@yahoo.com

Website: www.blessyourhealth.info

www.ingramcontent.com/pod-product-compliance
Lightning Source LLC
LaVergne TN
LVHW051846080426
835512LV00018B/3101